THE ART OF COACHING
VOLUME 1

The Six Figure Blueprint

Ryan Niddel

CONTENTS

Hello
my name is

INTRODUCTION

Introduction

STOP

Yes, You...

Read this before you begin the book!

This is <u>IMPORTANT</u>. I want you to buck the trend that is currently growing by the day. Bringing the epidemic to your awareness is the first step in changing it.

You are not going to finish this book (statistically speaking)

If New York Times best-selling "Thinking Fast and Slow" was only completed by 3% (or under) of the 2,000,000 + people who purchased it, chances are VERY low that you will read this book from cover to cover.

If that stat doesn't shock you, congrats...you are one of the 97% that don't finish books when they purchase them.

I want to change that for you, today.

I, very intentionally, did not add any "fluff" to the pages you are about to consume (which is ironic considering this sentence is considered "fluff" in a literary sense).

Each chapter has actionable steps (backed up with FREE support offered in an easy to access way) that are the exact steps of the blueprint that I have used to create a 6 Figure+ coaching business.

If you read that and think "well even a broken clock is right twice a day (congrats again you cynic), has anyone else actually implemented these steps and seen any sort of success?"

The answer is "YES!!"…and many at that!

(testimonials can be found here to support my claim – http://social.7fbs.com/humble)

I want to challenge you to begin to be honest with yourself (don't worry, I cannot read your mind and won't call you out on this ever)

Do you ever finish 100% of what you start?

If you answered "YES! Always" (I would say you are lying…but that aside) then you will read through this book, get to the resource guide at the end, and begin to make more money implementing all that works in this book.

If you answered "No" then I would encourage you to draw a line in the sand from this point forward. Today is the day you change that story. Today is the day where the success you have been searching for has finally found you. Today is the day that you read, learn, and implement what actually works.

If you are someone that "loves to buy, but hates being sold", I have some bad news for you.

There is no up-selling coming on the back-side of this book. There is no special offer "just for you". There is no promise of riches and wealth by doing next to nothing and waiting for the checks to role in.

There is a proven path that provides results, that when executed, will lead to a heightened level of success.

If you feel compelled, after reading this book, to explore other ways to increase your leads, your sales, and your free time…I would welcome a call with you.

Simply book It here – www.calendly.com/ryanstime/brainstorm

There are a few conditions for the call..

1). You DO NOT have your credit card near you during our time together on the call

2). You DO NOT try to beg me to buy something from me on the call

3). You DO come to the call focused on the largest hurdle(s) that stand between you and the success you crave and deserve.

4). You have a coaching/consulting/mentoring business that is currently generating revenue.

And from that place, I look forward to hearing how this book has grown your business and made a positive impact in your life.

To your unlimited success,

Ryan Niddel

CHAPTER ONE
WHAT I DO AND HOW I GOT HERE

CHAPTER ONE

What I Do And How I Got Here

I know where you're at my friend. You have big ambitions, big goals, big dreams and a big message to share with the world. As you start going down this path, the amount of information that comes at you can become overwhelming, can't it?

When you really look at it, everybody has a way to get you from point A to point B. The amount of advice you will be given can leave you reeling with information overload. While I won't say any of those other people are right or wrong, what I will share with you is taken from my personal experience. I'm going to go through my journey, step by step, with you, and share with you what it has provided for myself and my family (namely a business income of six figures plus).

I didn't start with a massive audience. I didn't have celebrity status, I didn't run any ads, I didn't pay for celebrity endorsement or anything like that. I was simply a guy that wanted other people to not feel the pain I used to feel. Which also happens to be my motivation for writing this book.

Like many people in this business, when I first embarked on this coaching business, I felt called and compelled to help everyone. Everyone that I came across could benefit from what I had in my back pocket. Age didn't matter. Socio-economic status didn't matter. The region of the world didn't matter. I was just someone aiming to help everyone, and I saw a LOT of people who needed that help.

One of my mentors, a man by the name of Kevin Nations, shared with me an impactful lesson. He said very clearly (in a slight Southern drawl, I might add) that if you try to be heard by everyone, ultimately, no one can hear you. It may be difficult, and it might even seem a bit counterintuitive to only speak to a handful of people. I can assure you, though, that it is one of the very best things you will ever do for your business, your relationships, and your sanity.

KNOW YOUR AUDIENCE

I'm going to walk you step-by-step through the process of how to contact and connect with your ideal client. No matter where you're at in the progression of your coaching, mentorship or consulting business, you will likely have someone who you connect with so deeply that you would spend time with them completely free of charge. These are people that you would gladly answer every time they call your phone. You will run into individuals that are just those "right" people. That's only natural.

When I first started my practice, I didn't believe there was a way I could only connect with people that I would naturally enjoy spending time with. It didn't seem possible that there was a way that only my ideal clients would want to use my service. I'm not only talking about my ideal clients but the "Unicorns" of my ideal clients. These are the ones that hit the "3M's". They have the mindset to decide to change and grow, they are motivated to act quickly, and have the money to afford my goods and services.

I couldn't have been further from the truth. As I began to speak clearly to my preferred audience, I noticed some profound results. With repetition and consistency came increased income and clarity. The same thing is going to happen for you. So the very first step to understanding how to get to $10,000 a month in recurring income from your coaching, mentorship or consultant business, is to understand your ideal client.

For our time together, we're going to refer to that individual as your Ideal Client Avatar (or ICA) for short. Your ICA is a person motivated to take action to change their life RIGHT NOW. By identifying your ICA, you're able to present the EXACT solution to solve their problem. They have the money it takes to invest in your time, product, and service, and they have the mindset to fully immerse themselves, loving every minute of what you are sharing with them.

IDEAL CLIENT AVATAR

Always keep the 3 M's in mind. Mindset, Motivation, and Money are the three ICA components vital for the long- term success and scalability of your business.

MINDSET MOTIVATION MONEY

CHAPTER TWO
DEFINING YOUR ICA

CHAPTER TWO
Defining Your ICA

The first 18 months of my coaching practice were spent trying to serve everyone. While that worked, and I was able to make much more than $10,000 a month, it was exhausting and tiresome. I was not serving the greater good of myself or my clients.

I would speak to anyone that had a pulse and wanted to be helped. And, the pulse was optional. I had many phone conversations with people that I thought to be potential clients, but they simply didn't fit. Some had the right mindset but lacked motivation. Some had motivation but lacked money. Some had the money but lacked mindset. All of those are recipes for short-term burnout and frustration. I speak from experience when I say it becomes very difficult to grow and scale your business while wasting time in that manner. My mission is to help you save time, energy, effort, and frustration while increasing your income and impact. Everything you need to accomplish this resides in this book and in your being.

As we look at your ICA, the very first thing we must do is humanize them. No longer can your avatar be a magical undefined name. We need specifics. Who do you coach — men or women? Perhaps the answer is both. Let's assume your business is just like mine, and you are 100% positive you can make a MASSIVE IMPACT in the lives of men and women. We will have to create ICA's for both. This includes names. We are creating a pathway to begin to think only in positive terms of our ideal clients.

We also need to know the ideal age range for our clients. Before you speed through this section, allow me to propose a question to you. Did you think the same way at 40 years old as you did at 20 years old? Probably not. The age range of your ICA needs to be a range where all participants would generally think the same way.

This is the first challenge of what I teach (that works). The part of your brain that feels compelled to help everyone will try to block this out. You will justify why it doesn't work. You will be afraid you will miss out on potential clients. To reach our goal we only need to serve 5% of the total market, but I will share more on that in just a little bit.

Now that we've defined gender, name, and an age range for your ICA, we need to take some time to determine the region of the world they live in. Will you serve a global market? Perhaps you enjoy regional reach a bit better. Maybe you simply want to dominate your local city. This is very important information to be aware of for the way you craft your messages (after all, someone in southern California probably doesn't speak the same way as someone from Wyoming). You need to know this for creating impactful messages your ICA can hear, as well as for the specific targeting you will use later on in your growth trajectory.

Perhaps you have never considered your ICA quite like this before. I understand. It's ok if it feels a bit overwhelming, even confusing. There are ample free resources available to you just for buying the book. You can find them at https://www.facebook.com/groups/the7figurecoach/. Just remember, not only am I setting you up to CRUSH the $10,000 per month threshold, but we are also laying the foundation for $100,000 per month as well.

LET'S DIG A LITTLE DEEPER

If you're on track so far, we now must specify the client's likes and dislikes. What are their five largest pain points that need to be solved? What type of books do they read? What Facebook groups would they be a part of? Who is currently their "guru" that they look up to? Are there any meetup groups they are a part of? What makes them jump out of bed in the middle of the night in a cold sweat? What gets them over-the-moon excited?

The deeper and more detailed you can go in answering these questions, the quicker and easier it will be to surpass $10,000 a month in earnings. There is no prize here for getting this task completed first. There will be a massive financial prize, and the gift of time, for you putting in the work on this right now. I recommend not progressing forward until you share all of the details of your ICA with the FREE Facebook group (https://www.facebook.com/groups/the7figurecoach/) for additional insights and clarity.

Success is your duty as well as your right. You have a world of people to impact. Don't let the pride of doing it all alone inhibit just how great it will feel to help all of those people, make all of that money, and work less than 20 hours a week.

ACTION ITEMS FOR "KNOWING YOUR ICA"

Here is a handy list of action items to make it easier for you to keep track of the information you will want to have ready before moving forward.

1. Know the ideal gender of your ICA – this is not who you have served, but who you want to serve.
2. Know the name your ICA – make it someone whose name has a positive connotation for you.
3. Know the age range of your ICA – not too broad, not too specific.
4. Know where your ICA lives – worldwide, regional, local.
5. Know what books/publications your ICA reads – who are notable characters here?
6. Know who the "gurus" are in your space to your ICA.
7. Know what wakes your ICA up in the middle of the night in a cold sweat – five things.
8. Know what makes your ICA incredibly happy – five things.
9. Spend time getting to sit in the seat of your ICA. What does it look like? What goes through their heads? There is no prize for rushing this.
10. Join The 7 Figure Coaches Corner Free Facebook group and post your answers for additional feedback and growth hacks. https://www.facebook.com/groups/the7figurecoach/

If you can answer all of these questions, your ideal client avatar should be very well established. You're ready to take the next step!

CHAPTER THREE
LEAVING THE PACK IN YOUR DUST

CHAPTER THREE
Leaving The
Pack In Your Dust

For now, let's assume that your ICA is as detailed and itemized as it can be. It's time to craft your Noise Canceling Message (NCM for short). This message is the way we separate ourselves from the pack. It's the way we cut through all of the clutter and the noise of the market and begin to establish ourselves as high-caliber leaders with a very clear mission. We have to make certain our ICA hears our NCM loud and clear. They will hear it in such a way that will seemingly speak only to them.

NOISE
CANCELING
MESSAGE

Right about now, you're probably thinking something along the lines of, "How do we do that? There are hundreds of other coaches I know, follow, and have heard of that do the same thing I do. How am I ever going to cut through the noise so that I'm the only one heard by my ideal client?" Am I right?

The answer is, we craft an NCM that speaks to the pain of our ICA while addressing the genius of being a problem solver. Don't let any part of this statement scare you off. I told you, these are the frameworks that will ensure you hit seven figures of income, as long as you are diligent, driven and consistent. Of course, it's difficult to make $1 million until you have mastered making $10,000. This message, however, will give you a tremendous jumpstart on achieving that initial goal of making $10,000 a month in recurring revenue for you and your business.

LET'S GET SPECIFIC

Now, in order to craft this NCM, we need to get specific and narrow down your ICA's, biggest frustration, their largest goal, and their most intimate desires. This ends up becoming the very core of your marketing message and will drive the creation of every product, every offering, every service that you put out in the marketplace. Your entire business model will be crafted around your NCM. There's no need to be overwhelmed here. I'm going to walk you through just how simple this is. Also, if you get stuck, lost or confused, reach out to the Facebook group for help. (https://www.facebook.com/groups/the7figurecoach/)

The irony of the NCM is its simplicity. 90%+ of the marketplace hasn't taken the time or invested the mental capital to figure out how to speak to the specific clients they can not only help, but want to attract. Having this crafted and committed to memory will place you in exclusive company with only the top 10% of your potential peers (I think you are in a league of your own, and I hope you begin to truly believe that too!).

THE COMPONENTS OF THE NOISE CANCELING MESSAGE

The NCM is broken down into three specific components.

Component 1 : Your ICA's Goals and Desires
Component 2 : Your ICA's Dreams and Aspirations
Component 3 : Your ICA's Pain Points

Component 1 : Your ICA's Goals and Desires

The first component is identifying your ICA's largest goal or desire. Think about the thing that they want more than anything else right now in this moment. I know that my ideal clients want to increase their income exponentially. What is the largest pain point that you are able to solve for your client? That should be in this part of your growth plan.

Component 2 : Your ICA's Dreams and Aspirations

Component number two is to answer what is their greatest dream or aspiration. This can be a little tricky. For some, their greatest dream or aspiration is often times confused with short-term goals. I'm going to encourage you to step back and think about what the greatest pain point in the world is that they want to solve for themselves. I know for me and my ideal clients, it's to work less, to make more money, to have more leads, and get more clients.
All of this is so that they can spend more time with loved ones. They want to make more money, but they want to work less hours. They want to work a lot less. And, they're petrified to say that out loud because most people look at them like they're crazy anytime they have stated that out loud.

Component 3 : Your ICA's Pain Points

The third and final component is to ask, what is their largest pain point or frustration? The largest pain point that I see inside of my ICA's life is that they're afraid if they're not showing up and working, their business is going to collapse and everything they built is going to disappear. This becomes important for you to be very clear on as well. There are a few things that I want you to consider as you're mapping this out. Remember to include variables that you can increase in a certain amount of time. You also want to focus on the large, overarching "why" of the pain point your ideal client is solving. You want to be incredibly specific to your ICA. This is a place where I see clients often get confused.

My advice to you is…Don't overcomplicate this.

You only need to be heard by a few because if not, you won't be heard by anyone. I have a template that I'm going to share with you that I would like you to begin with. Prior to improvising and trying to create something of your own word-smithing (which is certainly fine), getting something dialed in is important. We have to make certain that the base level is created prior to making changes. That format I suggest is...

I help _____achieve or do _____ so they can _____.

An example of this for me is:

"I help motivated coaches, consultants and mentors increase their income by as much as 300% in as little as 90 days. So they can spend more time with loved ones without fear of their business collapsing."

Isn't that clear? Doesn't that speak exactly to who it is and I want to serve? Doesn't that cut through all the noise?

I look at this as your one-floor elevator pitch. Imagine that someone hopped in an elevator with you and was only going down one floor. They say "Hey, I'm Ryan, nice to meet you", and you introduce yourself. They then ask, "what do you do for a living?" At that point, most coaches that I know would say, I am a _____ coach. I'm a life coach. I'm a business coach. I'm a holistic coach. I'm a wellness coach. There's nowhere else for that conversation to go other than for the companion in the elevator to say, "Oh, that's nice."

Now, let's rephrase that conversation. I say, "Well, I help motivated coaches, mentors and consultants increase their income by as much as 300% in as little as 90 days so they're able to spend more time with their loved ones, without having any fear of their business collapsing." The person in the elevator, can now start a conversation which can lead to conversions. Anyone that has told you something different has something to sell you.

I suppose I too have something to sell you.

I want to sell you your success. The success you crave. The success you so rightfully deserve. So, conversions happen in conversations. When they say "how do you do that?", that will lead us into our next training, which is referred to as your Ideal Client Avatar Signature Solution (ICASS). It is something that only you can offer, that will cut through even more noise in the marketplace.

ACTION ITEMS FOR YOUR NCM

So, for today, you need to get specific and narrow down the answers to these three questions.

1. What's your ICA's biggest goal or desire?
2. What's their greatest dream or aspiration?
3. What's their single largest pain or frustration?
4. Construct the "1 floor elevator pitch" that will leave the listener asking "how?"
5. Post your message in The 7 Figure Coaches Corner private facebook page for feedback on the quality of your message (https://www.facebook.com/groups/the7figurecoach/)

Example: I help dedicated fathers lose up to 30 pounds in 15 days so they can look and feel their best without giving up any of the foods they love.
Whatever it is that speaks to you and solves the biggest pain point for your ideal client will help cut through the noise that is the marketplace and help to zero in on the people you can help the most.

CHAPTER FOUR
YOUR ICASS IDEAL CLIENT AVATAR SIGNATURE SOLUTION

YOUR ICASS: IDEAL CLIENT AVATAR SIGNATURE SOLUTION

By now, you should be incredibly clear on exactly who you want to serve. You should also be clear on their pain points, where they spend time, and all the other variables we've covered so far. In addition to that, you should have your perfectly crafted message that cuts through the noise of that marketplace. That is your Noise Cancelling Message (NCM).

If you don't have your ICA and your NCM completely honed-in, STOP. Do not go further. Do not pass go. Do not collect $200. You need those two completed first. Similar to our lives, this book builds upon past experience. If you don't get clear now, you will only experience more confusion. If you are stuck at any point, for any reason, please join The 7 Figure Coach's Corner private Facebook group (https://www.facebook.com/groups/the7figurecoach/) immediately for help.

It is my goal to help you get to $10,000 a month in recurring revenue as quickly as possible. If you're stuck now and I do not know, I can't help you get there, because I won't know what trouble you are having. The 7 Figure Coaches Corner is a community, filled with high caliber coaches, consultants and mentors. There are also multiple live trainings each week as well as recorded custom training to get you through the hurdles that could exist inside your business currently.

It's a very powerful community with brilliant individuals that are all driving forward together, pushing their businesses to seven figures and beyond. So if you haven't joined yet, now is the right time. https://www.facebook.com/groups/the7figurecoach/

Now we're going to jump into something that I refer to as your Ideal Client Avatar Signature Solution (ICASS). This is what we're going to answer back when the person in that elevator says, "Wow, how do you do that?"

There's a very specific way to handle that.

Think of all the ways and all the different times people have asked, "How do you do what you do?" Maybe you say, "Well, I have my accreditation or certification from this place", or "I have this way to do it", but the message isn't clearly conveyed. Have you had that happen before? I think most of us have. So, the goal of the training and this step of the journey is to come up with something that is customized just for you. A response that speaks specifically to your ICA, who's already heard your Noise Cancelling Message, and now wants to know how you can actually pull it off. This signature solution will make you Google slap proof, and Google slap proof is not for SEO. It has nothing to do with backlinks.

What's the number one thing that most prospects will do to you once they understand what it is that you can do for them? Well, unless you found them in a peak emotional state, the very first thing they're going to do is Google what it is you're going to offer them. What's the best way to not be outmanned, outspent, or trumped by someone that's been in the industry longer than you have? Answer - Simply create terms that, when someone Google's it, you're the only result that shows up. I'm going to teach you exactly how to do that in just a moment.

The ICASS provides a significant competitive advantage for you, and establishes market distinction and domination. If you have this, your clients will always take great comfort in your unique ability to communicate and deliver the exact result they're in search of. What I want you to consider is that this is the exact opposite of monetization. The goal of this is to truly make you stand out as a market of just one. Creating a signature solution is rather simple. I would like you to write down everything that you have learned, everything you have learned from that old version of you until right now. Whoever the old version of you was, what would be the things that you wish you knew? Write them down to the best of your knowledge.

A GREAT PLACE TO START

Let me share an example with you for context. If I go back in time to before I started my coaching business, to a time where I felt called and compelled to make an impact in people's lives, there was a lot I didn't know. I didn't know about a Noise Cancelling Message. I didn't know about an Ideal Client Avatar. I didn't know about a signature solution. I didn't know about 18 other things that I needed to know (don't worry, I'll share with you in the course of our time together).

I wrote all these things down on a sheet of paper, in chronological order to the best of my ability. Then I saw which ones could fit under a unique (but specific) topic.

What is a "topic" you may ask?

Well, what is a topic that the old version of me, wishes that I knew? I wish I knew about avatars. Underneath avatars, I write down all of the steps that had anything to do with understanding, speaking to, or identifying avatars.

It takes me away from the fact that I was really frustrated and exhausted from trying to speak to everybody while not being heard by anyone. What did I want?

What was the desired outcome? What was the true goal? Well, the goal would be to be very clearly heard by a specific piece of the market.

So how do we create a specific topic that speaks to our ideal client avatar and is unique enough to be google proof? The ideal client avatar is the unique name that I have for all things avatar related.

You need to follow this process for as many steps as you can possibly come up with. What I find with most clients is they have somewhere between 27 and 90 things that they want to teach someone.

I love it when there are seemingly endless steps on a sheet of paper. That means there is deep thought, ambition and excitement. It means that you are coming from an authentic place.

That means you are thinking outside the box. Please keep in mind, we all have a bias for just how simple we believe what we do really is because we live it daily. The idea is to break this down to the ridiculous. Reduce it to the ridiculously simple. Every small step has value to it and, if every small step has value, then the only bad step to write down is the one that you forget. So give yourself ample time for this. As you write all these down, inevitably you will see that some can be pushed together in the same box as a topic.

That's perfect. We're actually searching for that very thing.

THE POWER OF THREE

There's a path to follow when you take someone from pains and frustrations to their goals and desires. What I have found to work most efficiently with the way the human mind processes events, is to come up with three groups of three to walk someone through. So, in my world, the first three steps are all based around focus. It's where you and I are currently located on our journey. We focus on who our ideal client is, we focus on how to speak to them, and we focus on what to sell them that solves their largest pain point.

The next three steps are growth based and zero in on how we begin to grow the business and the three after that are all based around scale. How do we scale the business so we're not trading time for money? Each one of those three words has three individual blocks (or steps, which all will have many sub-steps). Fairly easy, right?

In each one of those three blocks, I personally have three sub-blocks, and three bullet points. For me, each one of those three bullet points has somewhere around three additional sub-bullet points. Are you getting it now?

It's just the way we chunk things down to make them easier to digest. If I told you, for example, that you had to go through what is a total of hundreds of steps, it would instantly make you think, "Oh, it's too difficult." right? We like things to see easy and direct. My friend, this is actually very, very simple. It's even more simple when you see it all written out. I have an example for you on the next page of what this looks like.

A SIGNATURE THAT STANDS OUT

So we want to call your signature solution something that is unique to you. Mine is called The 7 Figure Coaches System because I actually have seven steps. Each one of those steps, (focus, grow and scale) has steps that only work in their own topic. Now, the scale only has two tiers to it, everything else has three. So I want you to consider when you write down everything that you have grown and everything that you have learned from the old version of you until now, and write it all out.

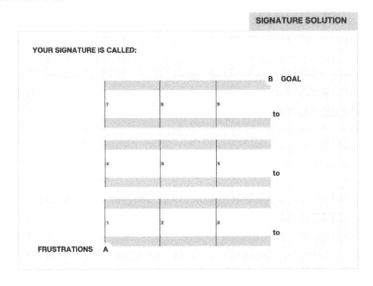

28

Make that list big with somewhere between 27, and probably 90 different things that you've come up with. Spend some time and extrapolate those. What were the frustrations and what were the goals that came from those? What is a Google slap proof name you can call that? I wouldn't want to call something "Facebook ad buying", because you could go and Google "How to Buy ads on Facebook" or "Facebook ads" and a bunch of other people would show up way before me. Either people that have been doing it longer or have spent more money and are just better at marketing than you might be. What you want to find is an easy to say, low search history, phrase on Google.

That's all.

That's the idea of your signature solution. So let's role-play this for just a moment, shall we? We're back in that elevator again. People hopped in, they press one floor down. We kind of roll our eyes that they were lazy and didn't take the stairs and say, "Hey, I'm Ryan." You introduce yourself and they say "So what do you do for a living?"

I say "I help motivated coaches, mentors and consultants to increase their income by 300% in as little as 90 days. So they can spend more time with their loved ones without fear of their business collapsing."

"Well, that's incredible. How do you do that?"

"Well, it's interesting you ask. I have something called The 7 Figure Coaches System, which has seven specific steps that walk you from being at a point in your business where you don't have clarity on where your clients are coming from, you don't have an easy sales process, and you don't have great time management.

It works you up to a point at which you're earning seven figures plus, and working fewer hours than you've ever worked before. We start by focus, we focus on your ideal client, we focus on your ideal message, and we focus on a way to cut through the noise. Then we start growing the business with simple sales processes, simple sales scripts and overall simplify every aspect of workflow. And then we get into scale, where we start to pull ourselves out of the business, and L.E.A.D (Leverage, Eliminate, Automate, Delegate)"

29

LEVERAGE
ELIMINATE
AUTOMATE
DELEGATE

Think about yourself for a minute how impactful that elevator interaction would be If instead of, "Oh, I'm a business coach." you rattled off what I just shared. Those two feel vastly different. Doesn't that make me instantly seem like an authority figure in the marketplace? Laughingly, I am one, but if I had just started, that adds validity and credibility to what I do. If you need to get this written on the back of a business card, or something to make yourself feel more comfortable, I encourage you to do it. Because this will change the way that the world shows up for you and that you show up in the world.

ICASS Action Items

So your action items from this training are to

1. Write down all the things that you have grown and learned since you felt compelled to create this business.
2. You're going to list your main topics for your solution - Ideally 9 are great
3. You're going to come up with a name for the solution that is specific to you, with low search history and no one ranking against you.

I have training on this available inside my podcast "15 Minutes To Freedom with Ryan Niddel" and free, ongoing weekly training, available on this specifically inside The 7 Figure Coach's Corner.   I would love to have you join the conversation.

So now we are really, really clear on who your ideal customer is, where they spend the most time, who the authorities are in their marketplace, how to cut through the noise of that marketplace, how to create a signature solution to walk people from where they're at to where they want to arrive, we must get very clear on an ascension ladder for them to walk themselves up.   This will help your ICA ascend through different pain points they experience.

The next step for us on our journey, is to begin marketing our products and services.

CHAPTER FIVE
BUILDING A CONTENT CALENDAR

BUILDING A
CONTENT CALENDAR

Now, keep in mind, this doesn't cost you any money, but it will cost you some time. The investment is certainly worthwhile, as just this strategy alone has provided myself and many of my clients with a $500,000 a year plus in income. So we're going to start with something that I refer to as a content calendar. How much easier would it be if you knew every day exactly what to post, how to post it, and why you are posting it? Currently, like most of my clients, what ends up happening is we get overwhelmed with the monotony of the day. We forget just how easy it can be to make an impact in the marketplace, and that's what the content calendar is all about.

MONDAY MONDAY

So we're going to start on Monday, and Monday is used for an engagement post. This engagement post should be typed, not a video or a picture. The engagement posts should fit in one of the nice colorful backgrounds on Facebook or on one page inside of Instagram. Typically open-ended questions are the best. For instance, "where would your favorite place to travel be if budget were no issue?" Things along those lines are used to spark conversations with your tribe and followers. Now, an important side note, you must engage with the people that are engaging with you.

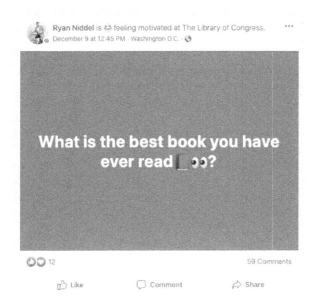

When someone shares where they would like to travel;

1. Like their comment.
2. Reply back to their comments and ensure that you tag their name in your response. The reason for this is that Facebook gives additional weight currently, at the moment of production of this book, to tags and conversations that happen in an authentic and organic manner.
3. End your response with an open-ended question where you look for information back.

My average Monday post with only 6500 followers reaches 3300 people. That's 3300 people that see my name pop up across their feed. That doesn't mean 3300 people respond. It means that 3300 people see what I have to say. What this also does is create the top of the waterfall that will cascade through the rest of the week. A bit of little known information for you - Monday, Facebook engagement is currently the highest.

TUESDAY TOO

So on Tuesday, we can almost guarantee any person that commented on our Monday post will also see our first post on Tuesday. That first post on Tuesday should be built around bringing your tribe closer to you. These are typically done in video format, preferably, and should be done using something called spark camera. This allows for the cut frame type of video that increases watch through time (the key metric for video relatability to your followers in Facebook's eyes). So, in order to bring people closer to us, we must share things that bring them inside of our lives. Perhaps it's what our superpower is, or something that we're still working on. Maybe it's a shout out to a close friend, family member or someone near to us. We're having conversations about our loved ones, or people inside of our business, but you want to insure that you are ultra-relatable to your Ideal client avatar. Also, please keep in mind that as coaches, mentors and consultants, we often times believe that we must have everything figured out. We don't. We are not suppose to. In truth, people most want to buy from people they can relate to. So make sure that your Tuesday posts are very, very relatable. These again should be video and format and should have a small caption that grabs attention.

WEDNESDAY WHAT?

Wednesday's post then is about giving away FREE value to the marketplace. The easiest way to establish yourself as an authority figure by giving away things that most people will charge for? Now, as you do this, this is not something to grab email addresses from. This is a real sharing of things that you know work. It could be something from your ICASS. It could be something from conversation with a current client. It could be something you have read that you implemented and know works. It could really be anything that adds value to your ideal avatar's life with nothing expected in return.

This too should be a spark camera video, three minutes or less in length, and should have an attention-grabbing headline and small type above the post. See reference for details.

ACTION THURSDAY

Thursday's posts will be the time in which we now ask for people to take action. We do this on Thursday for a number of reasons. First of all, most people in the world get paid every other Friday, so people are most likely to make a buying decision when their bank account balances are the highest. Second, throughout the week, the people that have become most engaged in our content are now the ones that are still seeing what we're sharing. So the closing percentage for them is going to be much higher. Third, we've established trust, authenticity, and brand awareness prior to putting out something to ask someone to take an action. These posts could consist of inviting people to a private group, inviting people to a low-end offer, inviting people to a mastermind, or inviting people to a case study.

I go very deep into this training inside of The 7 Figure Coaches Corner Facebook group. I would love for you to join us (getting tired of me trying to give away value yet? Don't be! I practice what I preach). There is just too much information that is constantly changing about best practices around posting, to articulate through a book. It could be a book unto itself (albeit an outdated one before it gets to the printer with the speed of social media these days).

FRIDAY PUMP IT UP

The Friday post ends up being specifically related to what you're looking forward to in the future. Perhaps it's someone you're looking forward to working with, or a trip you're taking, or a book you're reading, or a course you're creating that shows an ideal client that we're not just stuck in one position, but that we also care about what's going on going forward. These too, should be videos, three minutes in length or less using spark camera and typed with a small description above the post.

Now for extra credit, and really extra reach that I want to share with you, a secret I refer to as priming the pump.

When you first wake up every morning, set an alarm clock on your phone, or go to eggtimer.com and set a 15 minute alert. Then, for 15 minutes straight, you're going to hop in your newsfeed and as quickly but diligently as you can, you're going to like and comment while tagging the original poster on everything you possibly can. Every bit of information, every bit of knowledge, every bit of anything. You want to make sure you can communicate. The exception being sponsored content.

Sponsored content gives no additional weight and it's not worth the time to comment on it. This would also be a great time to start cleaning up your friend feed. I say that, because we're going to start treating this profile like a business in itself. In the next chapter, you're going to learn one of the biggest secrets to increasing engagement and increasing reach on Facebook.

IT'S THE WEEKEND!

So, Saturday and Sunday become free days, days in which you have extra time to post extra content of whatever comes to mind. No matter what, don't forget to prime the pump. Seven days a week, for 15 minutes. Like and Comment on every post. You can even make a game out of it, see how many you can get done each day. Over a 30-day period, your reach inside Facebook should more than double instantaneously. If during the same time you start eliminating people that will never do business with you, and only adding in the ideal clients you want to attract, can you imagine just how quickly your business will grow? I think you're starting to see how we're getting to the $10k a month in recurring revenue.

CHAPTER SIX
ULTIMATE HACKS

CHAPTER SIX

ULTIMATE HACKS

This chapter is a little bit different. We've set a lot of groundwork, a lot of foundation, gotten very clear on a schedule, who to talk to, how to talk to them, and how to walk people up the value ladder. Now let's talk about some ways to accelerate your growth. Someone even referred to this chapter as one of the ultimate hacks that exist in getting you to that elusive $10,000 a month in recurring revenue benchmark; to anybody that says that, I would have to agree.

This entire chapter is dedicated to the secret things that "they don't want you to know about in order to grow your business". They being the ones that require you to buy expensive software to grow your business. They being the ones that say you have to spend money on advertising in order to get in front of the right clients.

Friend Filter.io

In order to really press the gas pedal to the floor, I'm going to share with you $50,000 a month secrets. More specifically, how I have grown my business and helped multiple other coaches, mentors and consultants get $500,000 a year in earnings without special software, and without ads. The very first thing that you need to know about is a Google Chrome extension called friend filter.io. What friend filter.io will do is revolutionize the way that your personal Facebook page operates. If you're anything like me, there was a time in life when your personal Facebook page was the ultimate connection point.

You might have started out with friends and family, then migrated into potential social circles. As your life took its twists and turns you might have added potential dating partners. Then as your business progressed, you started adding more and more contacts of anyone that you thought could use your service. From this point, you probably are starting to see some of the fallacies in that decision. Your product, your service, your goods are now very specialized to 5% of the 5%. What that means is we have niched down in a market establishing us as true authority figures.

So instead of just saying coaches, you can now help life coaches that are men. That would be a sub-sector of an established market. If you have started a business already, you may have noticed that you have clients that have outperformed all the rest. Those are the kind of clients you want to attract more of. Those are the people we have to make certain are on that friends list.

What friend filter.io creates is a way to only connect with and only have people on your personal Facebook page that interact with your profile. If the people that interact with your profile are not your ideal client, that's okay. We're going to change that. What we're going to do first is download friend filter.io installed on our Chrome browser and execute its command. It's going to show us every person in the last 180 days that has interacted with our Facebook profile. Those are people who have liked one of our posts, have commented on a post, that have shared a post, or have entered into our direct message platform.

This is important because Facebook is throttling your delivery, based on the percentage of people that are interacting with your posts. They're doing this because Facebook wants to send more quality content to people that are interested in it and get rid of the stuff that people don't care about.

So the very first thing we need to do is to run friend filter, see who we've interacted with, and eliminate everyone that hasn't interacted with our posts. I can almost hear you from all the way here in Ohio, "But what about the people that would be offended that I unfriended them, like my grandmother, my great aunt, my long-lost brother?"

It's a great question.

Those people, you can put on a whitelist, which will never get removed. In order to grow, scale and maximize your business, you're going to have to start doing things that are a little uncomfortable. Comfort and complacency are the enemy of progress, and you bought this book in order to experience massive progress inside your business. I would never ask you to do something that I have not or am not currently doing inside of my own business. Running this program is the foundational step to begin to leverage your greatness and get in front of all the people that need to see it.

WHAT'S NEXT?

So we've run the friend filter, and we've eliminated every person that we can. Facebook will penalize you for removing too many people too quickly, so ideally you only remove a couple of hundred people a day. No more than two hundred. We do this because we want it to feel organic. For Facebook's algorithm behind the scenes, a normal person wouldn't be able to spend time unfriending a few hundred people. You want your behavior to feel the same.

Once you have unfriended the majority of the people that have never engaged with your posts, you'll rerun friend filter once every 30 to 45 days. We always want to be thinning the herd of people that don't engage with our posts. This, coupled with priming the pump from the previous chapter, will start to create a massive wave of new reach. But from here, we need more people to reach. The best way to do that is as follows.

When you think of your ideal client avatar, you know that they're part of separate groups and tribes. Those groups and tribes you should be a part of your strategy as well. Every day for 10 minutes, you should go into that group, and find the people that are most active in the group. You should request them as friends and genuinely care about what they're posting and sharing. Over a period of seven days, if you add or simply invite 50 people a day, you will have invited roughly 350 to your page, and roughly 175 will accept the friend request.

At this point, Facebook will start to only show you people in your "people you may know" section that mimic the online behavior of those people. The days of accepting friend requests from anyone that doesn't meet your ideal client avatar will have long gone. We will no longer accept new people that won't be someone that we would conduct business with.

It doesn't matter what the extenuating circumstances are. This is now business. You have a job to do! This is not a hobby. It's going to take consistency and diligence to the process in order to reap the maximum upside benefit. So every day you'll spend time in groups posting, commenting, sharing, and compiling a list of people to invite to your page. From that standpoint, once you have invited 50 people, you will invite a few more throughout the day.

From your "people you may know section" as friend requests get approved, you're going to spend time asking open ended questions, and getting your new friends to respond to your page. This shows Facebook that the connection was authentic and that the person really cares about what you have to say. Some good examples of this are as simple as, "Hey, [insert name]. I saw that you do this thing. Would you mind telling me more about it? I'm very curious."

Everyone likes to talk about themselves. Play up that aspect. If you believe that asking somebody about their business is too forward and too obvious of a tactic, ask them about the city that they live in. "Hey, [name], thanks for accepting my friend request. I see that you live in [insert city]. I've always been curious about what it would be like to travel there. If I made it, what's one thing you recommend that I should do?" We ask them something, only to get a response back. This triggers new activity inside of Facebook that shows that you're authentically connected.

Under no circumstances do you turn this into a pitch. This is simply a conversation like you're meeting a stranger at a local convenience store. If they eventually get to the point of begging you for your service, you can invite them to a call, which will be covered in a separate chapter. The goal here is to simply get to know them and be able to eventually be in a position to add value. If you question that this works, I have a question to ask you. Typically, do you want things that are easy to obtain? Or do you want things that are a little more difficult and out of reach?

Of course, you want things that are difficult and out of reach. So, why would you be "thirsty" and jump through hoops aggressively working to attain a client when no part of that makes it look like you're out of reach to THEM? You want to play "hard to get" by making it seem that you are so busy, so important, so impactful, that there is no way that you would ever consider working with just anyone. Ultimately, very soon, you're not going to have the time to talk to just anyone. So once we've run friend filter, once we begin to cruise new Facebook groups, we also begin to invite people to our page.

CHAPTER SEVEN

ADDING HUNDREDS OF PEOPLE

ADDING HUNDREDS
OF PEOPLE

Once we begin to have conversations back and forth with them, there's still more steps to take. Each morning, after you've primed the pump, take a little bit of time and go to brainyquotes.com. Brainyquotes.com will allow you to share quotes that will speak to your audience and also be great engagement starters. These quotes can be things that you should give credit to the original author, for this is another way to add value to the marketplace.

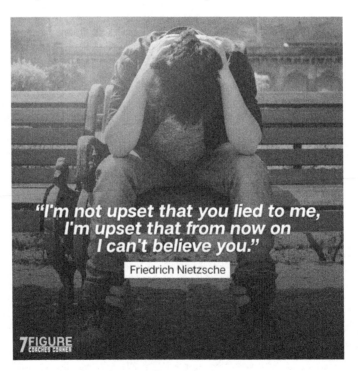

"I'm not upset that you lied to me, I'm upset that from now on I can't believe you."

Friedrich Nietzsche

7FIGURE
COACHES CORNER

Now that we are adding people, now that we have a system, we must make sure that your profile looks like something that people want to interact with. Unfortunately, what you want for your profile picture has almost no meaning here. Let's lay off the cat memes, and the posts of aunt Sally's Casserole. If we share a post that does not have meaning must interrupt people's eyes and makes them curious, and it should still speak to your ideal client avatar. So, if you're Ideal client avatar is married, business owning women, make certain your profile picture, your banner image, and all of your posts will matter to that person.

They need to make you a relatable authority figure.

Your profile picture should speak to your ideal client avatar and be something they aspire to become. We want to make it polarizing to the clients we wish to work with. The profile picture itself should be something that grabs attention.

The banner should be something that invites people to your group, which is coming up later in this chapter. You're going to need to create a Facebook group that speaks very clearly to your ideal client avatar. For instance, mine is The 7 Figure Coach's Corner. It is very obvious this is somewhere, where coaches, mentors, and consultants can come together to connect as a tribe and community. All of that is actually said in the base of my banner on Facebook.

From here there's a call to action that's physically on the banner itself. Click here to join now. When someone clicks it on Facebook, it will pop open the images and window and show the text next to it that you've entered as a post. That text will have a click here to join a link that pushes people to join your group. Pretty simple, isn't it?

The same thing needs to be the very first image in your carousel of thumbnail images. A call to Action with a "click here to join my group". We join a group because we can now start filtering people that are really interested in taking action versus people who are just interested in looking at it. This formula alone will allow you to create $10,000 a month just from your group. In addition to the banner and the profile picture, we have to make sure that your description is something that catches attention as well. Think of all the things that every other person post. Coach, mentor, fitness enthusiast. There's nothing wrong with those things, but they certainly don't cut through the noise, do they?

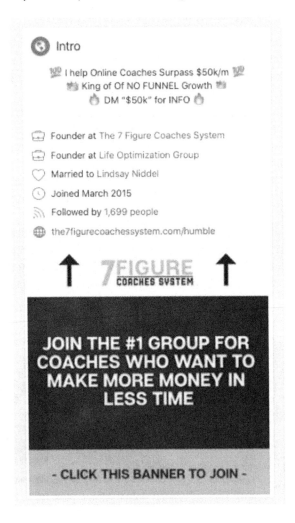

Not for me.

So, as you're considering what MIGHT cut through all that online noise, think of something that would have someone ask "what is that"? I have no more information about what that person does. The headline on mine at the point of recording this book is "I create L.E.A.D.ers". Because I know that I help coaches, mentors and consultants L - leverage their true brilliance, E - Eliminate the waste that does not serve them, A - Automate all of their business they can to free up time and mental space, D - Delegate what cannot be automated and that isn't in their genius zone.

That sort of statement is enough to get someone curious to scroll through my profile and get a better idea of who I am. As they're getting a better idea of who I am, they will also see my posts, the posts from the content calendar that speak to my ideal client avatar that doesn't feel like an endless sales pitch, which isn't what anybody wants to see. This process works. All of it is done very intentionally.

You must be intentional and start playing chess. While your ideal clients are playing checkers. Now, we also have to make certain that the link in our profile pushes people to our Facebook group and that we share enough personal information to feel relatable, but not so much to overwhelm someone. No one likes the busy profile that has everything someone has ever done in their life with every job, everything. It's overwhelming. Stay away from what is not important.

We also need to make certain that our Facebook profile is completely public. We want every person coming to the page to be able to see all that they care to see about us. Nothing hidden, nothing private. Nothing is off limits. Everything out there in the complete open. These tips, tricks, and hacks, when done consistently for 30 to 45 days, create guaranteed results.

Make sure you're consistently posting quality content and that you're consistently adding value to the marketplace. Also, you need to be consistently establishing yourself as an authority, consistently removing unengaged friends, and adding only ideal client avatars. If you are doing all of that, you will consistently cultivate people into your group or to your brainstorming phone call, which is covered in the next chapter.

Before we wrap up this lengthy chapter, we have to talk about your group for just a moment. Your group has to have a very simple name like we've already discussed, but there's another secret to how to maximize a group. You want to make sure that the group is private. It should never be public. Think about any nightclub you've ever been to or any sporting event. Anything that feels exclusive makes you feel special. It feels like getting behind the velvet rope.

EVERYONE WANTS TO FEEL SPECIAL

The same thing is true for your group. It needs to be private so that it feels exclusive. Facebook currently allows you to ask three questions of your tribe before entering your group. These three questions can have massive value in the future. The three questions I would have you post are as follows.

1. **Welcome to [group name]. We're excited to have you here! There is no shortage of [ideal client avatars] waiting to come into the group, so any incomplete request will be completely denied. Do you agree?**
   And then required next to it so people see it, the second question.

2. **What is the largest pain point that exists inside of your [ideal avatar] world?**

   For example, my question is, "What's the biggest roadblock inside of your coaching business? Would you like help moving it out of the way?" That is also required. As for the third question...

3. **Where can I send information and marketing?**

   The third and final question is aimed at getting their email address. I say, "Would you like a personalized video introduction?" which gives them answers to the first question that you know will make an impact on your ideal client avatar's life.

A FEW MORE HELPFUL ITEMS

The software that helps automate this process is called Group Funnels. Group Funnels integrates those three questions, compiles the data, and exports it into a Google Doc that then can be manually processed or added to a CRM. I told you you didn't need technology to pull this off, but a CRM will be something to consider investing in.

I use Active Campaign for a number of different reasons. HubSpot is also a viable option that is very inexpensive, if not free. Every time someone joins the group and you have their email address, and their biggest pain point, you're able to slowly provide them value through email to build authority, brand and eventually brainstorming conversations. This will be covered in the next chapter.

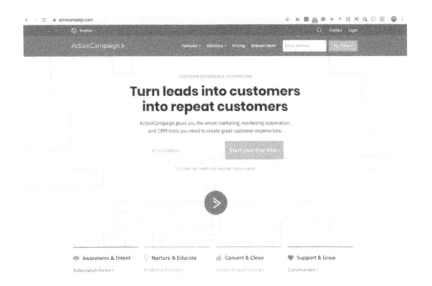

Now that we have the base level framework for the questions, we also have to cover what should be on the banner. The banner for your group should very clearly state who your ideal client is and the value they will receive from joining the group. This value should be clear, concise and simple. My banner reads "The 7 Figure Coaches Corner for coaches, mentors and consultants looking for more leads, more sales, and more time."

Very clear, isn't it? It speaks exactly to who's going to be in the group and exactly why they're there. It doesn't get much easier than that. Now, once we have the group established, we also need to have a cadence for the content in the group. I know this chapter is getting lengthy, but all of this information is well worth it. The more money you want to make, the more value there is in the problems you have to solve.

So, as you've looked at your avatar, hopefully the pain points you're solving are not things like, "I don't know how to tie my shoe" and are more like, "I don't want to go through the cost of an expensive divorce".

Why divorce, for example? The average divorce in the United States, at the point of writing this book, is roughly $25,000 to get completed. If there was a way to stop someone from going through a divorce, wouldn't that be worth $3000 - $5000, maybe even $10,000. Of course, it is but to tie someone's shoes, would be worth pennies. Be cognizant of this in your pricing tracking and the problems you solve for the avatar of your choice. Now, the best way to solve problems and create engagement in the group is to go live.

Facebook loves live content, because it's interactive, and it shows you're using the platform. I recommend going live no less than three times a week until you get your group to thousands of people. Yes, three times per week, and make it very obvious to people exactly what they're going to get when they come to the group. This will be in the welcome video, and the welcome post tied to the group. I have extra training available on this topic inside The 7 Figure Coach's Corner.

If you're curious about how to maximize your profile, it's far too much to share in this book. This is yet another section that could be a book unto itself.

Your Ultimate Hack Action Items

It has been a long chapter, but here is an easy list of your action items from what we've covered.

1. Download friend filter.io then run it and remove all of your unengaged friends.

2. Join groups where ideal client avatars are located

3. Add 50 people from those groups each day

4. Make certain to prime the pump every morning before you post anything

5. Have some of the first posts of the day be the most engaging, something like quotes from Brainyquotes.

6. Make sure that your profile has a
    *   unique profile picture
    *   a call to action banner and eye-catching description
    *   five great carousel pictures with the first being another call to action.

7. Create a Facebook group that has an easy name to associate with your ideal avatar

8. Make certain the banner on that page covers who should be in the group and the value they're going to receive

9. Ensure the group is private

10. Ensure the group has three questions, one of which addresses the client's biggest pain point and one is an email capture.

11. Make certain you have groupfunnels.com running behind the scenes to compile all that data.

12. Shoot a compelling video for the welcome video and have great content welcoming people to the group.

Do these things consistently for no less than 45 days and you will see the results of massive upside success.

CHAPTER EIGHT
THE BASICS OF TACTIACL APPROACH

The Basics Of Tactical Approach

Inside of every business, there are strategies and tactics. The first few chapters of this book were strategy-based. The previous chapter, and the next chapters to come, are tactics-based. Tactics are the way that you execute strategies that will generate revenue quickly. While we've built both strategy and tactics, I'm going to give you a secret formula.

Yes, this formula by itself has generated for me and my clients more than seven figures of income, without technology, without media expense, without anything other than a little well crafted posts. Those well crafted posts, I refer to as the SMS post.

WHAT IS SMS?

This is a way to draw attention from your ideal client who you've been building trust with over the last 35 to 45 days, while also cultivating a hungry audience waiting for the first opportunity to do business with you. The very first time I crafted this message and tested it, I generated 76 leads and converted it into $22,500 in monthly recurring revenue, almost instantly. That doesn't include the follow up and follow through clients that also joined me later. . Your results might not be the same, but they could be better.

The S stands for **small**, the M stands for **measurable**, and the final S stands for **specific**. That's the framework of this post. You're going to be looking for a small number of people looking to achieve a measurable outcome in a specific amount of time. It should be short, ideally with a colorful background filled with white words. This should not be a picture, but rather a type of post inside of Facebook, Instagram, or any other platform where you gain traction.
So let's craft an example of what a small measurable and specific post would look like.

I'm looking for:
- five motivated life coaches
- who want to increase their income by $10,000
- in the next 35 days or less

So we have a small number of people, just five, a measurable outcome being an extra $10,000, and a specific amount of time, 35 days.

This post should not be executed until you have at least five weeks of consistent content inside of your content creation calendar. You should also, after three weeks, have eliminated all of your old or un-engaged followers (in the first 3 days), and have been adding at least 30 new quality connections a day. That's as many as 600 people that could see your post. Not to mention the organic followers you already had.

Together, this creates a perfect storm of people that are foaming at the mouth, waiting for you to offer them something to help them because you've established consistency and authority in the market. We also want to put a disclaimer to remove people that don't fit on the post. When I say remove people that don't fit, think of the non-starters for you. In order to make that extra $10,000 you have to be willing to work at least three hours a day. You can't do that if they're not a good fit.

So you must have an extra seven hours a week to be able to handle managing a bigger bank account. You want the second part to be funny. Then you put in a call to action like "Pick Me below for more details." So after all of that, you put the post out and all together it would look something like this:

"I'm looking for five motivated, life coaches who are looking to increase their income by as much as $10,000 in as little as 35 days.
***Must have an extra seven hours a week and be able to manage a bigger bank account.

Comment "pick me" below for details."

Ryan Niddel is 😋 feeling happy.
November 14 · 🌐

🦄 Life coaches - would you like to generate a daily flow of leads...

(without ad spend, complicated funnels, or tech overwhelm).
Comment below and I'll give you he simple way FOR FREE!

Now, once that is posted, you will have already primed the pump that morning. You will spend 15 minutes just like every other morning, doing everything required to get to this moment. When you prime the pump, and you ensure the fact that you have the biggest opportunities for reach, you're going to post this almost directly after. Ideally do this in the morning, and remember that speed is your ally here.

As soon as someone comments and you get the notification, comment back, and tag their name in the response.

**You want to make sure that you're not saying the same thing to every person. Remember, Facebook likes authentic interactions and uniqueness. If you copy and paste the same thing over and over again, you're no longer unique. Now you might be asking the question, "What do I do next?"

I want to share something with you. If could 600 people that might now see my post, and If only 5% actually see it, that's 30 people. If only 20% of those take action, that's six people. If your product is $1500 a month, this post can make you $9,000 a month in recurring revenue, without technology without ad spending, and without having to hop on the phone. This is something that should not be deployed every week. This should be deployed once a month. Now that we have the framework down for the post itself, let's talk about what we say to them in the chat message.

WHAT TO SAY

This sequence must be followed exactly. Do not deviate from this under any circumstances or it will not work. This is tried and true and has been proven over and over again. Here's what it looks like. Someone comments, you exchange information, and you end up in their direct message. Now we're going to talk about what we say to them. The flow of this is always consistent. The very first thing we say to them is

Hey, [person's name] !!! [Enter]

I saw your comment on my post. [Enter]

Thank you so much for the engagement. [Enter]

The reason that we keep sending individual messages is because that's the way that we actually speak. It also, if they're on their phone or on their computer, will show three separate alerts letting them know there's some urgency here. At that point, we say nothing until they respond. Most people say "no problem", "Absolutely", "my pleasure". Now, we want to phrase it in such a way that we put ourselves in the authoritative role. How we do that is with the following.

Before I share all the details of what I've created with you... [Enter]

Would you mind me asking you a few quick questions so that I can see if you are a good fit for what I have created? [Enter]

Do not say anything else until they respond. Every person says "sure", but what you have done is put yourself in the driver's seat that little line that says "so I can see if you are a good fit". This also gives you an out at the bottom. Before you present what your offer is, hold back if they do not meet your criteria.

Every person I have ever found says yes. After they say yes, you share.
Wonderful! Thanks!

Every time that we ask for feedback from a potential client, we want to praise them. We want to have them feeling like they have done a great thing. We want them mentally feeling like they're seeking our approval. So we would start by asking for a success that they have now. If these are already established people, we talk about what that looks like for them.

We'll talk about my industry, coaching. I like to talk about where they want to arrive at first, because I want to have them in an elevated emotional state prior to bringing them back down to reality. So I would ask, currently, what is the next rung of the income ladder you're searching to grab on a per month basis? This is a fancy way of saying, "how much money are you trying to make?" People always answer,

"Well, gosh, I'd really like to get to $20,000 a month."

My answer is always:
"Beautiful!", "Excellent!", "Incredible!"

Then I say
"I have no doubt you'll get there. The only question is how quickly?"

That's when I instantly jump into the next question.
"Where is your current income sitting?"

They're going to share it. No matter what they share, I say

"I understand that. That's still really good money though."

Then I put it on them, and I ask,
"So what's the biggest hurdle standing between you and $20,000 per month?"

They're going to share whatever they share with you. When they share it, you respond back with:
"I understand"

Most people that I get the opportunity to speak with share something very similar. Respond with:
"I'm very familiar with that."
and then you ask a question,

"Would you like an easy way to get those hurdles out of the way?"
People always say "Yes", right? They've told you their pain point. "I don't know how to generate sales.", "I don't know how to generate leads.", "I don't know how to close someone.", "I don't have enough time."

People always say "yes". The next question we ask is
"OK, moving those obstacles out of the way. Would you like to wait and do it later Or do you like to jump on it sooner?"

This is testing someone's wherewithal to jump in to get behind the scenes. Everybody I've ever spoken to says they definitely want to move it out of the way now, and I congratulate them.

Perfect. I had a feeling you were a quick action taker. That's great! It sounds like you're the perfect fit for my program. [Enter]

You wait for them to get excited, and say "yay" or "good". Then you play takeaway.

Instead of breaking my thumbs and trying to type in all the details, I've saved the notes of what I have created in a simple document. [Enter]

I hope that's okay. [Enter]

There's no fancy funnel, or anything beautiful to look at. [Enter]

Are you okay if I send it over to you to look at right now? [Enter]

Everyone says yes. They've already felt like they've closed a deal. They're almost to the point of being able to get what you have to offer them.

It's coming right up. But do me a favor, open it up and read it all the way through. [Enter]

I'm going to sit here with my chat window open until I hear back or in case you have a question. [Enter]

Then send them the document that you've created to outline your program. If you'd like more information on how to create this document, join The 7 Figure Coaches Corner where I break down exactly how to make this document happen. This would be an entire book on its own, so instead of trying to cram it into this book, I've created a course for you to be able to digest it in a much easier format. At the end of the document that you have created, there is always an option to say they're all in to jump into the program. So when someone's done reading the PDF, all that's left is for them to either ask a question or say I'm in. Let's assume that they say they're all in.

You congratulate them on making a great decision, tell them that's wonderful, tell them how excited you are.

Now let's get you quickly enrolled into the program.

However you get people into your program, maybe you have your own online platform, maybe it's a Facebook group, whatever it is you want to get them ready.
"By the way, what's the easiest way to pay for whatever the program is?"
"Are you okay if I send you a link right here and wait for you to pay it?"

People will say "yes", then we must give the link to them right now. Then we sit here and we wait for them to jump in. During this time, I also ask

"what's your best email address?"

I need their email address now to send them a few consistent documents (like my love it or leave it guarantee where if you're not completely satisfied with the outcome that you get, you will get 100% refund on the product).

Every person that decides to work with me also gets an expectation sheet. There are 13 things you can expect from me, and I only expect three in return. That's created to show people that I am bringing more to the table than I require my clients. Then, depending on the level of service you decide to work with me, you might also get the next year's content calendar. In that you get invited to the masterminds that we have three times a year in Columbus, Ohio. You also get invited to the three calls a week that we have to help you progress in your business and you get access to a whole bunch of bonuses.

That's the best way to handle that situation because it shows someone how serious you are about this craft. From there, you can invite them into your group. Hopefully you have a private group specifically for your members inside of Facebook, and you share a welcome post. You take their picture from their profile, tag them in it, and you share it across the board. You welcome them to the group, and you get people to comment, and you make them feel bonded and a part of the tribe and community. These things create such an impact and they didn't require you to pick up the phone.

More Action Items

In the next two chapters, I'm going to cover the basics of selling by phone. You're going to get the script and the format that works every time. Your action items from this chapter are as follows:

1. Create an SMS post that is small, measurable, and specific. It should have exclusionary side notes to invite people to have conversations through chat.

2. Do not post links in Facebook. Not in your posts or in your comments. Facebook throttles the response of your post.

3. Go through the chat format that was provided in this chapter. Do not deviate from that format.

4. Ensure you have a PDF or document ready prior to getting into a chat conversation and then sit back and watch the money roll in.

Every time that I post this, I get at least four new clients. What would it be worth to you if every time you post you get four new clients paying you monthly recurring revenue? How many months would it take you to get to $10,000 in recurring revenue? I bet if you're honest, it would only take you two months of consistency to get to that level. Consistency is the key word, though. Every step up to this point you must do with ruthless consistency in order to reap the benefits of what's in front of you.

SETTING UP AND MAKING SALES CALLS

CHAPTER NINE

SETTING UP AND MAKING SALES CALLS

This chapter is another tactical training session in the process of hitting your first $10,000 a month in recurring revenue. I have a proven and specific framework that creates sales without selling. It breeds and environment with your ideal client avatar where they know like and respect you, while asking you if they can work with you (how is that for selling)?

See, most people in the sales world seem to rush into trying to close people. That is backwards to everything that you should actually do in order to create demand in the client's mind. So, with that being stated, what is it that you must do in order to build massive demand and make it easier to close sales? I believe a multi part, short framework, sales call cycle is most advantageous.

Nobody wants to hop on a call where they feel sold. Everybody will hop on a call where you come up with solutions to help them with their biggest problems. In order to book this call, I use something called calendy.com.

Calendly is an appointment booking software that allows me to have control over when, where, and how I have conversations with potential clients. I choose to run a two-day setup for my calls. Let me explain what that means. This goes back to our conversation about exclusivity. When given a choice between what they can always have or what is difficult to have, we've already determined that people want what is more difficult to acquire, or things that are exclusive.

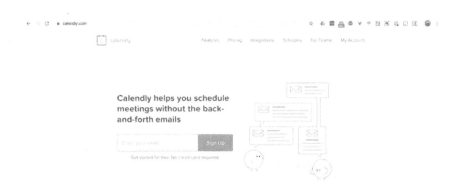

We never want to make ourselves too available to hop on a phone call. As you're starting out, this is going to feel strange because you're hungry for closings. You're hungry for sales. I get it, but trust me, this works. What we need to do is to establish a way that you have calls only with ideal clients, and only at times that serve you. Here is the format for these first phone calls.

The calls are exactly 15 minutes. 15 minutes means 15 minutes. It doesn't mean 20, it doesn't mean 30, it doesn't mean five. It means 15. The reason for this is that we have to make certain that we don't make ourselves too available to a client on this call. It's natural in a coaching business to want to solve clients' problems. That is not the purpose of the brainstorming call. The purpose of the brainstorming call is to brainstorm. Yes, this client is potentially the right fit for your business. They won't know it but you're still brainstorming to see if they meet your criteria. Not every client is a good fit for your business, so quit trying to make them so. What we're going to do on this call is set the framework for what's to come in future conversations.

CALENDLY IS YOUR FRIEND

Much of this framework that I share with my clients mimic the sell by chat covered in the previous chapter. It still works so no need to recreate it. So, let's first discuss Calendly a little more in depth. We have to use Calendly as a way to hold time and space on our schedule, allowing you to determine what windows of time are available for potential clients to book time on your calendar.

I only allow calls on Tuesdays and I only have them from 10:15 in the morning until 6:30 at night. That's it. Every call is 15 minutes and there's 10 minutes of wrap-up time after every call. This allows me to take notes, to get my head clear, to eat, to drink to use the restroom, and do anything else I would have to do to ensure that I'm ready for the next call. Your first goal should be to 100% book out 1 day on your calendar.

It's going to take some time to get there, but once you do, you'll thank yourself later. The best way for us to do this is when we put out emails, say that if they require a one-on-one brainstorming session, click here. Inside that brainstorming session they can only book on a certain day on your calendar. That's good and normal. When they go to book time on your calendar, there are going to be a series of questions that you ask them. Those questions that you ask them are as follows.

First, what is the main problem your business solves? Or what is the main problem that you're looking to overcome? The second question is what the largest roadblock is currently in the way of your success. Third question, are you open-minded to solutions to solve whatever the problem is that you have? If anything on this investigatory conversation comes back in any way other than exactly what you want, it's okay for you to email the client and say we're simply not a good fit. You do not have to waste your (or the potential client's) precious time having conversations that don't turn into sales with your ideal client avatar.

We are not able to waste time if we are to truly grow and scale a business. It simply doesn't work. We must always remain focused on why it is we are doing what we're doing. Now from this place, we can talk about the structure of the phone call itself. This phone call has a very specific cadence, tone and excitement level associated with it. We must make certain that we show up with one level more energy than the person on the other end of the phone. That sets the tone for the fact that we're always on and that we have something just a little bit more than they have available to them. They're searching for that and they're going to require it from you in order to make a buying decision. Don't show up tired, lethargic, or worn out for these calls. It's not going to help you close anyone.

Now, on this call, we're going to have complete control of the conversation from start to finish. The very first question that will set the exact cadence of this call will be as follows. First, you're going to call them exactly at the time that is committed to, not a minute or two late. Integrate Calendly with your calendar and you'll never miss a call.

CHAPTER TEN

YOU'RE NOT ALONE ANYMORE

CHAPTER TEN
You're Not Alone Anymore

So here we are. You've now established the exact framework that I have used for myself and hundreds of clients to get them to and far surpassing the $10,000 a month recurring revenue model. Now, I must say that while this book provides real solutions to problems every coach faces, there are plenty of other solutions out there and the book itself will consistently be updated with the help of The 7 Figure Coach's Corner, private Facebook group.

By now, you should see that this book, while adding tremendous value, is also designed to assist with getting people to join a tribe and community. If you have received any value from this book at all, I would heavily encourage you to come over and join the conversation inside The 7 Figure Coach's Corner. The reason for this is that we have tremendous amounts more work to do.

This book works whether you're already past $10,000 a month, or you're just in the process of getting there. In the group we cover more in depth topics, all complimentary. We do so to ensure the fact that you experience the success that you ultimately deserve. I'm a firm believer that if I give away as much value as possible, the right clients will reach out and want to work hand-in-hand with me. Potentially at this point, you're one of those clients. I'll make it very easy to do so.

The link to spend more time with me one-on-one is calendly.com/ryanstime/brainstorm.

Yes, knowing that you came from the link in this book actually matters because you'll already have all the pieces and parts to ensure success. In addition to being able to have a one-to-one phone call with me to establish how I might be able to help you grow, I also host three mastermind meetups in Columbus, Ohio, where we get tactical, not strategic.

At these meetups, I have copywriters, content creators, videographers, sound producers, graphic designers and much, much more there at your disposal to ensure that when you leave the two-day event you have deployable tactics already in play. This mastermind has no pitches associated with it. You come to learn to network and to grow. I also have a podcast, on which I give away tons of valuable information. It's all completely complimentary. You can access the podcast by searching for *15 Minutes To Freedom* on your favorite podcast player.

In addition to the podcast, the mastermind, and a one-to-one phone call, we also have the ability to spend time together in my weekly mindset matters group phone call. Potentially your business is already exceeding expectations and it's just the mindset of what can go on that has you stuck. You're not alone, my friend. I've been there hundreds of times before and I'm sure we'll be there hundreds of more times. Easy way to move past that is to work with the tribe of mentors to ensure your future success that can be found at https://www.facebook.com/groups/the7figuremindset/. This is a PAID group. It is $97 per month, but the first call is completely free to jump on!

CHAPTER ELEVEN
ADDING VALUE
TO A LIFE

CHAPTER ELEVEN

ADDING VALUE TO A LIFE

Now that I have all of the pitching out of the way, I have some more value that I'd like to add to your life. We've covered a lot in a short period of time. This book was designed to add value while providing lead generation. How impactful would it be for your business to establish yourself as an authority by writing your own book?

The framework is much easier than you might have ever believed. The framework that I'm going to share with you is something that I took from the great and wise Dean Jackson. He has a theory called The 90-Minute Book, which is how this book was written. The 90-Minute Book premise is as follows: sit in front of a sheet of paper, a whiteboard or your computer screen and share bullet points from your signature solution. In those bullet points, have sub-topics that can also be added. These should not be well thought out or very lengthy. They should be more of an overall synopsis. With the fact that you now have a signature solution, this should become very simple.

I have shared with you just a few steps of the first three steps of my signature solution. Can you imagine what the next steps could be? Of course, more value and more impact. When you itemize the steps to your signature solution on a board there should be between 7 and 10 or 12 steps. At that point, pull out your phone, put in your earbuds or whatever it is that you use to communicate with the outside world via phone calls, and begin to record yourself speaking about each one of the topics at hand. Each topic should take between 10 and 15 minutes to discuss.

This will follow a very logical flow because it will be just like you're talking to a potential client. From that standpoint, take these audio recordings that are saved to your phone and upload them to a transcription service. I use otter.ai. It's $10 a month for 600 minutes of transcription. Once you upload it to otter.ai, you then take the transcription and export it into a Word document.

From that Word document, you read through it and add as much as you can to expand upon the points that you shared. This can be done in a very simple time effective manner over the course of a few days. Once you're somewhere between 20,000 and 25,000 total words, you'll be in a position to send it over to a copywriter and editor. Those can be found on upwork.com as well as many private Facebook groups, or even something as simple as fiverr.com. Once a copywriter and editor has worked through the book and made it something that is enjoyable to read, you now have a framework to become a published author.

Upwork

In-demand talent on demand.™
Upwork is how.™

Upwork expertly connects professionals and agencies to businesses seeking specialized talent.

Get Started   Get a Demo

Julia B. | Top Rated Writer

| Web Dev | Mobile Dev | Design | Writing | Marketing | Accounting | See all 80+ categories |

Proven talent
Access the world's largest talent network – with visibility into every review.

Flexible scope
Tackle short-term, longer-term, and complex jobs.

Enterprise-ready
Safeguard with comprehensive compliance services and results risk limitation.

---

fiverr

Graphics & Design   Digital Marketing   Writing & Translation   Video & Animation   Music & Audio   Programming & Tech   Business   Lifestyle   Industries

Hi Bearlyfly,
Get offers from sellers for your project

Post a Request

Flyer Design
Promote your business with printed marketing materials

Made on Fiverr by magicllas

Recently Viewed & More

See All >

ndmarjawaid821	yashge95	sep_eight	chehdal6	begantbushkola
I will edit pdf files, combine files, organize pages	I will edit PDF document professionally	I will do PDF editing with required specs	I will combine merge convert pdf files into single file or...	I will convert format PDF files to epub
STARTING AT $5	STARTING AT $5	STARTING AT $50	STARTING AT $5	STARTING AT $5

Best Sellers In Convert Files

Potentially being published may not be in your wheelhouse currently. You still will need to track down a graphic designer for the cover and potentially some good quotes for references, but you now have your signature solution inside of a lead magnet that can be given to people that are curious about what it is that you do. Let's be honest with each other for a second, shall we?

Think of all the PDFs and all the ebooks you've ever downloaded. How many of them have you read from cover to cover multiple times? If you're anything like me, that answer and percentage is very, very low and very small. So the idea of this is to provide a tremendous value while at the same time, establishing yourself as an authority figure. This is a part of my equation that I refer to as the authority amplifier.

More importantly, if recording through your headphones doesn't seem to make sense to you and you've always wanted to launch a podcast, this is the perfect way to begin. Each episode can simply be a podcast that you can still get transcribed through otter.ai, and then you turn it into a multiple point conversation. I trained my clients on a specific methodology to take every piece of content that you ever created and get three value added touch points out of it, and an automated system that allows you to create an impact in the marketplace.

This is just one of the many tactics that I have up my sleeve. If you were to join The 7 Figure Coach's Corner, or the mastermind, or book your one-to-one phone call, you'll see there's never going to be a bad time to have a book. There's never going to be a bad time to have a podcast.

Our mind simply overcomplicates what we believe to be very difficult. I've taken immense pride in figuring out the shortest, simplest ways to get the maximum amount of things done for myself and for my clients on a daily basis. That's why I can say with complete confidence, that if your desire is to work under 30 hours a week, there is a very simple systematic format to pull that off. Some of it comes down to systematization, some of it comes down to delegation, and some of it comes down to elimination, all of which we can work on together.

Once you have your transcriptions, and your copy written and edited book back, once you find your graphic designer to design your book cover. You can use that for lead generation as a lead magnet, or ship it over to Amazon for printing on demand. These things happen so efficiently that every specific niche of your marketplace should have a book from you to them to establish your authority.

Imagine, if you will, that instead of handing out a business card or handing out some brochure or pamphlet, you hand out a book. Not sure about you, but I don't recall the last time I threw a book away. I simply don't do it. I may not read every book, but I never throw them away. So when you create something like this and you get it in the hands of your potential buyer, your potential client realizes it might not turn into an immediate sale, but long term it starts to fill up your pipeline very nicely. Just like I hope this book, at this point, has done for me.

Made in the USA
Middletown, DE
24 January 2020